DATE DUE

REG	DEC 31		
BOH	JAN 21		
ASE	FEB 26		
WE9	MAY 02		
KJ11	DEC 10		
MEL	FEB 10		
CB11	FEB 25		
NPY	APR 02		
JT	APR 12		
EB7	MAY 0		
GLG	MAY 11		
JH11	MAY 24		

Your Teeth

by Helen Frost

Consulting Editor:
Gail Saunders-Smith, Ph.D.

Consultant:
Karen Masbaum Yoder, RDH, Ph.D.
Indiana University
School of Dentistry

Pebble Books

an imprint of Capstone Press
Mankato, Minnesota

1

Pebble Books are published by Capstone Press
818 North Willow Street, Mankato, Minnesota 56001
http://www.capstone-press.com

Library of Congress Cataloging-in-Publication Data
Frost, Helen, 1949–
    Your teeth/by Helen Frost.
    p. cm.—(Dental health)
    Includes bibliographical references and index.
    Summary: A simple description of the basic structure of teeth, the various types,
and the difference between baby teeth and permanent teeth.
    ISBN 0-7368-0115-4
    1. Teeth—Juvenile literature. [1. Teeth] I. Title. II. Series: Frost, Helen, 1949–
Dental health.
    RK63.F76 1999
    611'.314—dc21
                                                                98-6989
                                                                   CIP
                                                                    AC

Note to Parents and Teachers

This series supports the health education standards for how to
maintain personal health. This book describes the types of teeth, the
parts of a tooth, baby teeth, and permanent teeth. The photographs
support emergent readers in understanding the text. Repetition of
words and phrases helps emergent readers learn new words. This
book introduces emergent readers to vocabulary used in this subject
area. The vocabulary is defined in the Words to Know section.
Emergent readers may need assistance in reading some words and in
using the Table of Contents, Words to Know, Read More, Internet
Sites, and Index/Word List sections of the book.

Table of Contents

4

Teeth have different
shapes for different jobs.

top incisors

bottom incisors

Incisors are the front teeth. Incisors have sharp edges. People use incisors to bite food.

canine tooth

Canine teeth are next to incisors. Canine teeth have sharp points. People use canine teeth to tear food.

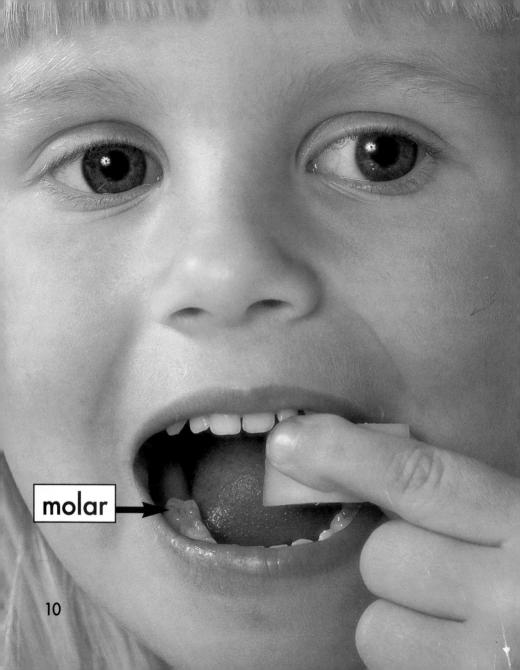

molar

Molars are the back teeth.
Molars are wide. People
use molars to chew food.

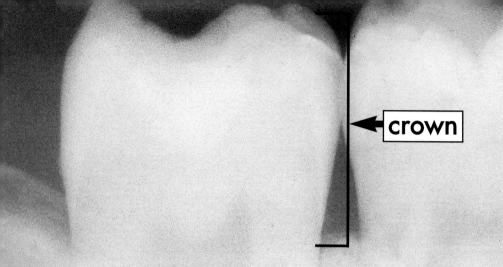

crown

The part of a tooth that people see is the crown. Enamel covers the crown. Enamel makes teeth hard and white.

13

gums

14

Teeth grow out of gums.
Gums are firm, pink skin.

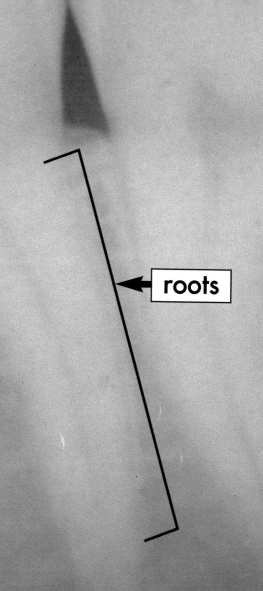

roots

Roots hold teeth in people's mouths. Roots are under the gums.

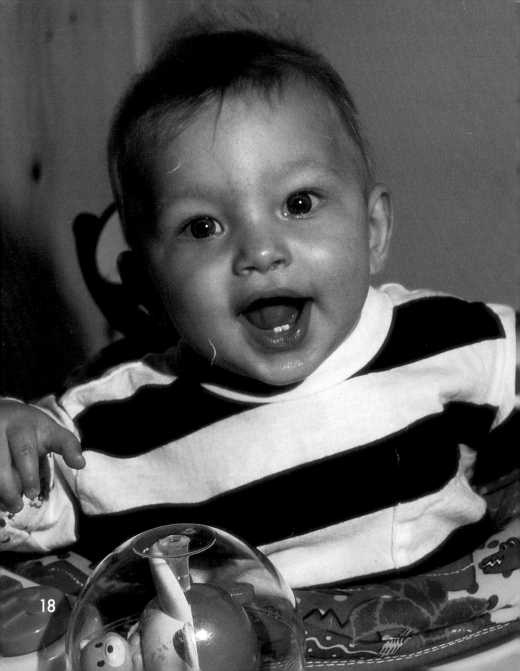

People get their first teeth
while they are babies.
Baby teeth become loose.
They fall out.

New teeth grow. These teeth are permanent teeth. They will not fall out. Most people have 32 permanent teeth.

Words to Know

baby teeth—the first set of teeth that grow; babies start getting baby teeth when they are about six months old.

canine teeth—pointed teeth that help people tear food

crown—the part of a tooth that people see

enamel—hard matter on the outside of teeth; enamel makes teeth white.

gums—the firm, pink skin around the base of teeth

incisors—the front teeth; incisors have sharp edges that help people bite food.

molars—wide teeth that people use to chew food; molars are in the back of the mouth.

permanent teeth—teeth that grow in after baby teeth fall out

root—the part of a tooth that holds it in the mouth

Read More

Gillis, Jennifer Storey. *Tooth Truth: Fun Facts and Projects.* Pownal, Vt.: Storey Communications, 1996.

Showers, Paul. *How Many Teeth?* A Let's-Read-and-Find-Out Book. New York: HarperTrophy, 1991.

Internet Sites

American Dental Association Kids' Corner
http://www.ada.org/consumer/kids/index.html

Anatomy of a Tooth
http://www.umanitoba.ca/outreach/wisdomtooth/anatomy.htm

The Teeth
http://kauai.cudenver.edu:3010/0/nutrition.dir/teeth.html

Index/Word List

babies, 19
baby teeth, 19
canine teeth, 9
crown, 13
edges, 7
enamel, 13
food, 7, 9, 11
gums, 15, 17
incisors, 7, 9

jobs, 5
molars, 11
mouths, 17
permanent teeth, 21
points, 9
roots, 17
shapes, 5
skin, 15
tooth, 13

Word Count: 131
Early-Intervention Level: 8

Editorial Credits
Colleen Sexton, editor; Clay Schotzko/Icon Productions, cover designer;
    Sheri Gosewisch, photo researcher

Photo Credits
Barbara Comnes, 20
Craig D. Wood, 10
David F. Clobes, 1, 8
Dwight R. Kuhn, 14
Nancy Ferguson, 6
Photophile/Chris Buhlmann, 18
Unicorn Stock Photos/Joel Dexter, cover
Visuals Unlimited/Mark E. Gibson, 4; John D. Cunningham, 12, 16